In honor of Jan and Don Wolverton and Dottie and Marshall Hill:
You helped me find my way in life, and I will always be grateful.
—K.W.

For all those who give thanks, all year long.
—R.P.

Mary's First Thanksgiving

An Inspirational Story of Gratefulness

Kathy-jo Wargin
Illustrated by **Robert Papp**

ZONDER**kidz**

ZONDERVAN.com/
AUTHOR**TRACKER**
follow your favorite authors

Mary looked out the schoolhouse window. The leaves had fallen, and every tree stood bare against the late autumn sky. The little black stove kept the room warm and cozy.

Most days, Mary was happy her family had come to live in America. But not today. She felt lonely and missed her best friend, Elizabeth, back in Ireland.

Mary's father was thankful to have his job shoveling coal, even though it was very hard work. Now Mary and her family had a little bit of food in the cupboard and enough wood to keep warm.

When the bell rang, Mary gathered her books and started for home. She could hear other children talking about Thanksgiving. Tomorrow they would be feasting on turkey and pie with friends and family. Mary knew the most her family would be able to put on the table was extra bread with honey and perhaps a sausage or two.

When Mary got home her mother asked, "What's troubling you?"

Mary didn't answer.

"I have a surprise for you, Mary. Mrs. O'Connor brought us a gift."

"I don't want any pie," she cried. "I don't want to live in America. We don't have turkey. We don't have any friends. There is nothing to be thankful about."

Mary felt a pinch in her heart when she looked up and saw her father standing in the doorway. Before Mary could apologize, her father spoke.

"Mary, I want to tell you a story. Long, long ago, a sailing ship fought stormy seas to come here. The passengers were from England, seeking a new life of freedom just like us.

"The colonists arrived in late December. Cold and hungry, many became sick and died.

When spring came, those who remained were eager to start planting. Sadly, they soon realized the seeds they brought from England weren't right for this new land.

"Their Native American neighbors offered to help by showing them how to grow crops and where to find food in the land around them.

"The colonists were grateful. It was a time of peace and friendship, and there was plenty of food to eat.

And when autumn came, they were so thankful that they planned a celebration with their new friends. For three days they feasted on venison, geese, corn, beets, beans, grapes, and chestnuts."

"But Father, life got better for them," Mary said softly. "It is still hard for us. We only have a few things to eat, and I don't have any friends."

But you see, not long after the feast they realized that they had not stored away enough food for the oncoming winter," Mary's father continued. "Each person was allowed only a small amount of food each day so it would last.

"The next season their crops failed. For months they survived only on clams, fish, and groundnuts … and a few kernels of corn a day for each of them.

One hot day the colonists came together to pray for help.

"The next morning it began to rain. God had answered their prayers! For the rest of the season the crops flourished, and more ships arrived with food and supplies. The colonists gave their thanks to God.

It is said that years after that celebration the colonists placed five kernels of corn on their plates to remind them of the hardships they endured. They gave thanks for the blessings each kernel represented.

The first kernel represented the beauty and bounty of autumn. The second kernel represented their love for one another. The third kernel represented their love for their families. The fourth kernel represented their friendship with the Native Americans. The fifth kernel represented their freedom to worship God without fear."

Our life in America may not be perfect, Mary," her mother added, "but there are many blessings we can be thankful for … like the O'Connor family."

"I'm very thankful for Mrs. O'Connor's pumpkin pie!" Mary's father said. "Next year at Thanksgiving there will be more food at our table, but this year I'm thankful for what we have."

I'm thankful for the love the three of us share," Mary's mother continued.

Mary's father added a fourth blessing. "I'm grateful that in America we can worship God without fear."

"Mary, surely you can name one thing you're grateful for," said her mother.

Mary thought for a moment. "I am thankful that Hannah O'Connor smiles at me. It makes me feel like we are becoming friends."

Well," Mary's mother laughed. "Our five things are very much like the colonists' five at those first Thanksgivings."

"You're right, Mother," said Mary. "When I see Hannah at church on Sunday, I will tell her the story of the five kernels, and that I am thankful she wants to be my friend."

In 1820 at the bicentennial celebration of the landing at Plymouth Rock, Daniel Webster, a well-known Boston lawyer, spoke about the hardships the Pilgrims endured and how they changed the course of the nation. At the banquet that followed, five kernels of corn were placed at each setting.

This tradition has taken root in homes across the nation. The five kernels remind people of sacrifices made by the first colonists during what later became known as "the starving time." Most of all they are a reminder that Thanksgiving is a time for reflection and gratitude.

Mary's First Thanksgiving
Copyright © 2008 by Kathy-jo Wargin
Illustrations © 2008 by Robert Papp

Requests for information should be addressed to: Grand Rapids, Michigan 49530

Library of Congress Cataloging-in-Publication Data

Wargin, Kathy-jo.
  Mary's first Thanksgiving : an inspirational story of gratefulness / written by Kathy-jo Wargin ; illustrated by Robert Papp.
    p. cm.
  Summary: Mary misses her life and friends in Ireland and is sad that her family cannot celebrate Thanksgiving Day the way their New England neighbors do, until her parents share a story of the Pilgrims' first harvest festival.
  ISBN-13: 978-0-310-71179-7 (hardcover)
  ISBN-10: 0-310-71179-7 (hardcover)
  [1. Thanksgiving Day--Fiction. 2. Immigrants--Fiction. 3. Irish Americans--Fiction. 4. Family life--New England--Fiction. 5. New England--Fiction.]
I. Papp, Robert, ill. II. Title.
  PZ7.W234Mar 2008
  [Fic]--dc22

2006005638

Editor: Betsy Flikkema
Art direction & design: Sarah Molegraaf

Printed in China

08 09 10 11 • 8 7 6 5 4 3 2 1